Judy,

Friendship...
Much appreciated,
believe me. Thanks for
being there. Thanks for
Being.

Best-
Sandee
Dec. 1989

Friends

Marcia & David Kaplan
Art by Phil Mendez

*The material in this book has
been compiled over a long period
of time. Many of the sources are
unknown to the compilers. We wish
to acknowledge the original
authors whoever they may be.*

This book is dedicated to true friends,
who can see right through you
and still enjoy the show.

Friendship?
Yes please.

...Charles Dickens

According to recognized to recognized aeronautical tests, the Bumble Bee cannot fly because of the shape and weight of his body in relation to his total wing area. The Bumble Bee doesn't know this; so he goes ahead and flies anyway.

A smile is a curve
that very often
can set a lot
of things straight.

Poise
is the art
of raising
the eyebrows
instead of the roof.

Friends in your life
are like the pillars
on your porch.
Sometimes they
hold you up,
and sometimes
they lean on you.
Sometimes it's
just enough
to know
they're standing by.

When the storm clouds come in, the eagles soar while the small birds take cover.

*In the long run
the pessimist may be
proven right,
but the optimist has
a better time on
the trip.*

*Give a man a fish,
and he can eat
for a day;
teach a man to fish,
and he can eat
for a lifetime.*

*Don't let
the good
things
of life
rob you of
the best things.*

...Maltbie D. Babcock

The happiest people are those who discover that what they should be doing and what they are doing are the same thing.

WORDS MAKE A BETTER WORLD

Honesty, workmanship, faith, education, charity, courage, responsibility, love, friends.

Everyone won't agree to this, but think how much better your life could be if just one person would…
YOU!

We act as though comfort and luxury were the chief requirements of life, when all we need to make us really happy is something to be enthusiastic about.

...Charles Kingsley

Success is never final
and failure never fatal.

It's courage that counts.

GIVE—

To your enemy, forgiveness.
To an opponent, tolerance.
To a friend, your heart.
To a customer, service.
To every child, a good example.
To all men, charity.
To yourself, respect.

I have always been delighted at the prospect of a new day, a fresh try, one more start, with perhaps a bit of magic waiting somewhere behind the morning.

… J.B. Priestley

Praise is
like champagne;
it should
be served
while it is
still bubbling.

*Happiness
is like a butterfly.
The more you chase it,
the more it will elude you.
But if you turn
your attention to other
things, it comes and
softly sits
on your shoulder.*

…Nathaniel
Hawthorne

The mind is like a parachute. It only works when it's open.

*The sound of
laughter is
the most
civilized music
in the world.*

*A certain amount
of opposition
is a great help to man.
Kites rise against,
not with the wind.*

...John Neal

*Use what talents you possess;
the woods would be very silent
if no birds sang there except
those that sang best.*

...Henry Van Dyke

*The highest reward for
a man's toil is not
what he gets for it
but what he becomes by it.*

…John Ruskin

*A critic
is a man
who knows the way
but can't drive the car.*
...Kenneth Tynis

May each of you get what you want out of life, and still want it after you've gotten it.

In referring to a friend—
You may not be in a class
by yourself, but it sure
doesn't take long
to call the roll.

...Bum Phillips

Few of us get dizzy
from doing too many
good turns.

The foolish person seeks happiness in the distance; the wise person grows it under his feet.

...James Oppenheim

The best way
to get rid of an enemy
is to make him
your friend.

The only way to have a friend is to be one.

…*Ralph Waldo Emerson*

Trying times are times for trying.

The Golden Rule of Friendship —

Listen to others as you would have them listen to you.

Enthusiasm is the electricity of life. How do you get it? Act the way you want to feel.

The impossible is often untried.

Observe the postage stamp; its usefulness depends upon its ability to stick to one thing until it gets there.

You must take a step
before you can
walk a mile.
Ten percent
of something
is better than
100% of nothing.

*Man does not live
by bread alone.
Sometimes he needs
a little buttering up.*

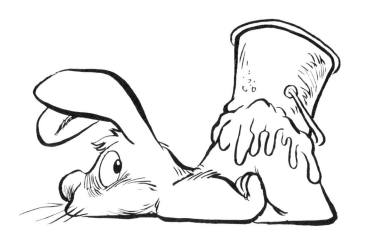

*When you're falling
on your face,
you're actually
moving forward.*

May the most
you wish for
be the least
you get.
May the best
times you've ever
had be the worst
you'll ever see.

FRIENDSHIP!

*a word the very
sight of which
in print makes
the heart warm.*

...Augustine Birrell

Life is the most interesting thing I ever got into; I'm glad I didn't miss it.

...*Adlai Stevenson*

*Add life
to your years
while you add
years to
your life.*

*The real secret
of happiness
is not what you give
or what you receive;
it's what you share.*

All is perspective.
To a worm,
digging in
the ground
is more relaxing
than going fishing.

...Clyde Abel

*There is a destiny
which makes us brothers.
None goes on his way
alone; all that we send
into the lives of others,
comes back into our own.*

...Edwin Markham

*What we see
depends mainly
on what we
look for.*

*One of
the greatest
sources of energy
is pride in what
you are doing.*

*The creation of
a thousand forests
is in one acorn.*

...Ralph Waldo Emerson

*For every minute
you are angry*

*you lose sixty seconds
of happiness.*

..Ralph Waldo Emerson

*Get someone else
to blow your horn
and the sound
will carry
twice as far.*

Sustained enthusiasm is life's most precious habit, life's healthiest attitude.

No distance of place or lapse of time can lessen the friendship of those who are thoroughly persuaded of each other's worth.

...Robert Southey

*Those who say
it can't be done
shouldn't interrupt
those doing it.*

*The gem
cannot be
polished
without friction
nor man
perfected
without trials.*

...Confucius

*There are
1440 minutes
in every day.
Make the most
of each one.*

Do more than exist—
LIVE!
Do more than touch—
FEEL!
Do more than look—
SEE!
Do more than hear—
LISTEN!
Do more than talk—
SAY SOMETHING!

…John Rhoades

*Friendship
is like
two clocks
keeping time.*

Opportunity ALWAYS looks bigger going than coming.

If my mind can conceive it, and my heart can believe it, I know I can achieve it.

*Before you
can hit the jackpot,
you have to
put a coin
in the machine.*

…Flip Wilson

Everyday comes bearing its gifts— untie the ribbons.

...Ann Ruth Schabacker

*If everyone swept
his own doorstep,
then the whole wide
world would be clean.*

*Because life
is short,
it's wise
to make it broad.*

*Patting a fellow
on the back
is the best way
to get a chip
off his shoulder.*

The best
we can do
is our most.

Leadership is…
courage to adjust mistakes,
vision to welcome chance,
and confidence to stay out
of step when everyone else
is marching to the
wrong tune!

A friend is one who takes you to lunch even though you are not tax deductible.

When your work speaks for itself, don't interrupt.

...Henry J. Kaiser

*A friend
is like an eagle;
you don't find them
flying in flocks.*

*Sympathy
is never wasted
except when
you give it
to yourself.*

If you sow kindness,
you will reap
a crop of friends.

Anyone who thinks he knows all the answers isn't up to date on the questions.

…Frank Lawrence

*Thanksgiving comes
but once a year,
but reasons
to give thanks
are always here.*

Friendship is
a special place.
I'm glad
we are there.

*It isn't necessary
to believe
in miracles.
Just hope
a few believe
in you.*

...Rod McKuen

Think

and you won't
sink.

..B.C. Forbes

*perience is
a hard teacher
because she gives
the test first,
the lesson
afterwards.*

...Vernon Law

*A little levity
will save many
a good
heavy thing
from sinking.*

...*Samuel Butler*

Diplomacy
is the art
of putting
your foot down
without stepping
on anybody's toes.

...Franklin P. Jones

*Applause
is the only
appreciated
interruption.*

Which shall it be!
Go! Go! Go! or
No! No! No!?

Express an opinion, but send advice by freight.

...Charles Clark Mum

Because it is common sense doesn't mean it is common practice.

*We are
all created
with an
equal
opportunity
to become
unequal.*

*Laughter is feeling
good all over
and showing it
in one place.*

*To find
a real friend
in a lifetime
is good fortune;
to keep him,
a blessing.*

*The gold of friendship
is a magic thing.
The more we
spend it on each other,
the richer we become.*